I0022708

M. A Meredith

Theotokos

The example for women

M. A Meredith

Theotokos
The example for women

ISBN/EAN: 9783337331443

Printed in Europe, USA, Canada, Australia, Japan

Cover: Foto ©Thomas Meinert / pixelio.de

More available books at **www.hansebooks.com**

THEOTOKOS

a

THEOKOTOS

THEOTOKOS

THE EXAMPLE FOR WOMAN

BY

M. A. MEREDITH

LONDON

KEGAN PAUL, TRENCH & CO.

1, PATERNOSTER SQUARE

1882

(All rights reserved.)

TO

LADY AGNES WOOD

THIS HUMBLE ATTEMPT TO LEAD THE

DAUGHTERS OF ENGLAND

TO STUDY THE CHARACTER OF THE EVER-BLESSED

THEOTOKOS

IS DEDICATED BY HER SISTER-IN-CHRIST,

M. A. MEREDITH.

S. MARGARET'S,
TONBRIDGE WELLS,
Festival of the Annunciation, 1882.

THE author of this little book desires to record her deep sense of the interest which the Venerable Archdeacon Denison has taken in its object and contents, and to express her grateful thanks for all his kindly help and wise counsel. She also wishes to state that for some of the thoughts embodied in the following pages she is indebted to the Rev. E. B. Pusey, D.D., the Rev. Sir J. E. Philipps, Bart., and the Rev. Isaac Williams.

THEOTOKOS.

THE EXAMPLE FOR WOMAN.

———◆———

THE writer of this little book ventures to hope that she may contribute something towards directing profitably the thoughts of members of the Church of England to the position which God has assigned to the Blessed Virgin Mary in the economy of grace; for as in days gone by the ever active, speculative mind of man, not content with the revelations made of the "highly favoured" of the Lord in the Holy Scriptures, searched too curiously into that wondrous life which the Church primitive guarded with such care, so in

later times the revelations which God has
by the Holy Spirit vouchsafed to man
have been too little studied, and the lessons
which they must have been intended to
teach have therefore remained unlearned.

No incident in the life of the Virgin
Mary, recorded in that book which God's
living witness and teacher has given to us
for guidance and edification during our
school-life here on earth, can be left un-
studied without loss; and the daughters
of the Church in England can learn
much that is specially needed in these
days of ease and luxury—days in which
freedom in thought and deed reigns every-
where, and the wise discipline of an earlier
age is almost unknown—by meditating
upon the character of her who was chosen
by God to be the Mother of His Son;
for that meditation will teach them what
is the true character of womanhood, and

what are the attributes of woman that find favour with God.

In dealing with any portion of God's word in order to learn a special lesson, it is well to remember that when we open the sacred volume we are, as it were, entering the presence-chamber of its Author, the great King, who is the same yesterday, to-day, and for ever; and that it is meet and right to make some preparation. It was said to one of old time, " Put off thy shoes from off thy feet, for the place whereon thou standest is holy ground." And what less can the children of the Church do than kneel before the throne of grace and pray for light to guide them in their search for truth?

The history of the Church, from its foundation to the present day, proves how prone man is to trust to his own imaginings; how, if he turn to the right hand or to the left, he may go on century after century in a wrong direction, each advancing step taking him farther from the centre of Truth. The great lesson which this fact illustrates is, that it is as dangerous to take from as it is to add to the written word of God. The Church in England unfolds the sacred Scriptures, and bids her children search for and learn what is contained therein; and in those Scriptures will be found all that it is God's will they shall know of S. Mary on the shore of time.

When meditating upon the life and character of the Blessed Virgin, we seem to rise into an unknown region, and to breathe an atmosphere of intense purity and infinite calm. The Revelation announcing the fulfilment of the promise of the Incarnation is unspeakably awful; and the more devoutly it is contemplated the greater appears the presumption of

man in trying to throw aside the veil
cast by the Creator round the Mother of
Him who was called "Wonderful, Coun-
sellor, the Mighty God, the Everlasting
Father, the Prince of Peace." To withdraw her from the still, secluded path
whither the Holy Spirit led and guided
her,—to enthrone her whose life is, save
on a few rare occasions, literally hid with
Christ in God, before the world,—is to do
what God has not done. To remove her
from the high eminence on which God has
placed her, and hide all those attributes
with which she was endowed, is also to do
what He has not done. He, the Omniscient, has cast a veil over S. Mary; but
He raises it from time to time, so that we
may learn to love and try to imitate her
who received not the grace of God in vain,
and who, submitting herself to His will,
was henceforth an example for all women.

The first vision which the inspired writers give us of the Virgin Mary is a glorious one, and the Church brings it before her children every year on the Festival of the Annunciation. This festival is one of those days in the Christian year which has an ever-recurring freshness and brightness all its own. It comes to us each year, as the ages roll on, when the days are lengthening and spring flowers are opening ; winter is past, summer is at hand, and midway between the darkness and the light stands the Feast of the Annunciation.

The shadows which had accompanied man from the day when he fell in Eden, began to disappear when the Angel Gabriel stood before the Lily of Israel and hailed her as the " highly favoured " of the Lord ; and when that " Holy Thing " which was born of her, revealed

Himself to man, light spread over the world. But man has loved darkness rather than light; for in that world this festival day of the Church—our Lady's Day—is remembered chiefly as a quarterly division of the secular year, and the men of the world are busy with its pleasures and its merchandise.

The children of the Church gather themselves together to do honour to the Mother of their Lord, and to learn the lesson which the Church would teach them when she points to the Virgin Mary in her lowly home in Nazareth. Her name was prophetic of her destiny in time and in eternity, for Mary means both " exalted " and "bitter;" and what human intellect can grasp the measure of her exaltation— the chosen one among countless millions —whose flesh was to clothe Deity; or what human heart can feel all that S.

Mary's did, when the sword pierced through her soul, and the great God In-carnate, who for thirty years had been to her a loving and dutiful son, hung upon the Cross of Calvary?

The record of the Annunciation is as grand as it is simple. We are told of the mission of an Angel to a Virgin whose name was Mary. The appointed hour had come, all things were now ready, the mandate went forth from the Eternal, and Gabriel stands before the Jewish maiden. The Messenger of God appears; and the daughter of David to whom he has been sent receives, as the daughter of a king, the greeting of the messenger of the King of Heaven. Pure, spotless, and undefiled she stands crowned with humilty before the Angel, as he utters the words, "Hail, thou that art endued with grace!" Human reason cannot fathom the depth of the

Angel's salutation to S. Mary; we cannot add to it, and we may not take from it.

The mind grows confused when attempting to understand the perfection of a created being whom God Himself by the voice of an Archangel proclaimed to be "endued with grace"—grace to which no limit is assigned. True it is that no limit can be assigned to the overflowings of God's grace, either to individual Christians or to those who, living in darkness in any age of the world's history, have no means of seeing that light of which the Baptist gave witness: but in these latter days, when the world is growing old and sin abounds, we seem so very far away from the "pure in heart," at such an immeasurable distance from the love and the faith and the courage which were grouped around the foot of the Cross of Calvary; and the lives of men and women are so

different now to the lives of those who
formed the "noble army of Martyrs" in
earlier days, that before meditating upon
the stupendous fact that a descendant of
the first Adam was found meet to be the
Mother of the Second Adam, it were well
to pray that we might be kept from pre-
sumptuous sin, and that we may catch a
portion of the Virgin's Spirit.

The Holy Scriptures teach us that the
fruits of the Spirit are love, joy, peace,
long-suffering, gentleness, goodness, faith,
meekness, temperance; and as we know
that with the Son, God freely gives all
things, and that He will withhold no good
thing from those who love and obey Him,
so we know that all gracious gifts must
have been abundantly bestowed upon her
who was to be the Mother of that Son.
In S. Mary was found the willing mind to
receive, and the loving, pure heart in which

to enshrine the gifts of God, and so by those gifts was she made ready for that greatest Gift, which she received when the fulness of time had come. The "princely spirit" with which her ancestor, King David, prayed that he might be stablished—stablished the highly favoured daughter of the House of Israel, and made her what she was when the Angel Gabriel stood before her and uttered the first " Hail Mary."

No daughter of earth was ever so adorned with rich gems, as was the lowly Virgin with jewels out of the treasury of heaven. She stands alone among the daughters of Eve as the chosen one of God, and what God had made her, and what she was in His sight, that she was in the sight of the Archangel; hence his salutation. " To Mary alone," says S. Ambrose, " was this salutation reserved. For she alone is well said to be full of grace, who alone hath attained such grace as none other hath done, to be filled by the Author of Grace." In her own eyes she was the "handmaid of the Lord," living to do His will, and willing that all His will should be accomplished in her.

When we realize in a measure all that being proclaimed "Blessed among women" involves, we begin to see what she, the favoured daughter of Israel, must have been. Taught and guided by the Holy Spirit, the benediction of the great King of heaven and earth rested upon her; and as He by His Spirit has thus presented her to our view in the shadow of His almighty wings, we may, with profit to our souls, gaze upon her and listen to the words which fell from her lips, and from those of the Angel in the Annunciation scene of the great drama shadowed forth in type and figure and predicted by prophets through a period of four thousand years, now to be acted on the stage of this world before the eyes of men.

Tradition, handed down through successive generations by holy fathers, teaches us that S. Mary was alone, praying in her chamber, when the Angel Gabriel appeared before her. She had been prepared for whatever honour God might confer upon her, when He bestowed the fulness of grace, and made her meet to become the Mother of His Son, by special gifts and graces of the Holy Ghost. Hence her dignity, hence also her humility, surpassed only by that of the Eternal Word.

It may be that the Angel knew that she, to whom he had been sent, was that one of whom holy men of old, inspired by the Spirit, had written as "The Beauteous Throne," "The Enclosed Garden," "The Sealed Fountain," "The Mystic Gate for ever shut," "The Rod of Aaron," "The Fleece of Gideon," "The Tabernacle," "The Ark," "The Spotless Lily," "The Cedar of Libanus," "The Tree of Life," and "The House of Gold;" for he had come into her presence by the command of God to announce the wondrous mystery of the Incarnation to her who was chosen to be the Mother of the Only-begotten of the Father; and we can imagine with what reverence the Messenger from the Court of Heaven must have saluted this chosen vessel.

"Hail, thou that art highly favoured, the Lord is with thee, blessed art thou among women," were the words which fell upon the ears of the wondering Virgin.

We are told that she was troubled at his saying, and cast in her mind what manner of salutation this should be. And Gabriel, seeing that in the depth of her humility she could not comprehend the height of her exaltation, added, "Fear not, Mary, for thou hast found favour with God. And behold, thou shalt conceive in thy womb, and bring forth a son, and shalt call His name Jesus. He shall be great, and shall be called the Son of the Highest; and the Lord God shall give unto Him the throne of His Father David, and He shall reign over the house of Jacob, and of His kingdom there shall be no end."

"How shall this be?" was the simple earnest question, prompted by a sense of Virgin purity, in answer to the announcement from Heaven; and the Angel replied, "The Holy Ghost shall come upon thee, and the power of the Highest shall overshadow thee; therefore also that Holy Thing which shall be born of thee shall be called the Son of God."

The message from the Creator was

delivered, and the Angel stood before the lowly Jewish maiden awaiting her reply. There must have been silence in heaven as the legions that surround the throne of the Most High listened for the Virgin's answer. Soon it came. "Behold the handmaid of the Lord, be it unto me according to thy word."

The curtain falls suddenly on this wonderful scene. Gabriel waited, as it were watching, until the words, which proved how entirely this blessed one felt that she belonged to Him who made her, fell from her lips; but no sooner were the words spoken, than the Angel departed from her, leaving her in the same attitude of expectant watching as our Lord left His disciples on Mount Olivet, when He ascended to heaven.

At this point in the sacred narrative the words, "according to your faith be it unto you," naturally recur to the mind. The Virgin Mary's faith in the omnipotence of God was perfect, and therefore, as it would seem, her waiting time for the descent of the Holy Ghost upon her was but for a moment. Henceforth and for ever she was in a position of glory to which no other created being could attain; her name, Theotokos; and her nearness to God un-imaginable to us, who by reason of our infirmities so often allow sin to come between ourselves and Him : it may be a little sin—pardoned for Christ's sake, even as the words, "Father, forgive," leave our lips,—but still they come, those little sins, and leave us, while they last, a little further off from God.

It has been well said by an aged saint that "What has been cannot cease to be; she who was the Mother of God-man, must be His Mother still; little were it to be the

Queen of Angels; the special place of the
Divine Mother must be in the special light
of her Divine Son." And before the curtain is drawn aside to disclose the next
scene in the story of the Cross, it may be
noticed that the Blessed Virgin by rightly
using the gift of freewill subjected herself
to Divine influence, and by freely making
God's will her own became *Dei Genetrix*,
the cause of her own salvation and that
of others.

For to deny S. Mary, as some have
done, the freedom of choice given to each
reasonable being, and to represent her as
merely a *physical* instrument of the Incarnation, is to lower her infinitely below all
God's great saints; for they attained sanc-
tity by subduing the passions of fallen
human nature, and overcoming the temptations of the world; or, to use the words
of S. Paul, by "bringing their bodies into

subjection." They willed that the higher part of their nature should rule the lower, and, by God's grace, and with His aid, the spirit of man gained the victory. Still, in their case there was the struggle—the resistance of venial, if not of mortal, sin · to the ever-flowing grace of God; hence this warfare which S. Mary avoided, by never resisting the outpouring of God's free Spirit upon her.

So it was that she was "full of grace." She was this because her will was in perfect and entire submission to the will ot her God. If she were not what the Holy Scriptures teach us that she was, by co-operating with the Divine Will—not by a fatalism which was final and unalterable, but of her own free will—then she was less than the least of the Apostles and Martyrs and Saints of all ages, who have fought against the World, the Flesh, and the Devil, and who, having gained the victory on the battle-field of earth, will be crowned in heaven.

But the Lily of Israel never roughly shook off the dew from heaven which was continually falling upon her, therefore she never knew what it was to feel parched and dry. She never opened her petals to the scorching rays of this world's fires, therefore they were never drooping under the weight of penitential tears ; her fragrance went forth, and because it was uncontaminated by aught opposed to the will of her Creator, it was as sweet incense before the Lord, and was accepted at the throne of Grace.

S. Mary must therefore be regarded as the first among God's saints, and the most striking illustration which the sacred records give us of the full meaning of the words, "Perfect love casteth out fear."

Daniel fell as one dead at the appearance of Gabriel, and it was only when reassured by the Angel's salutation, "O man greatly beloved!" that he stood on his feet and listened to the revelation which God sent His messenger to make known unto him. S. Mary knew no fear, because, through entire obedience of the will, her natural weakness was *perfected* in God's strength.

From her we may learn the fearless strength and power which love and obedience give to woman—a power which each ought to strive after by co-operating with the Divine Will. From her we learn what self-renunciation really means — a lesson which was never more needed than in this latter end of the nineteenth century. Self-pleasing, self-exaltation, selfishness in every form and phase abound : self-denial, self-abasement, self-renunciation abound also, but as exceptions to the general rule, and in the aggregate would probably be found an equivalent to the "few chosen" among the "many called."

Where one daughter of the Church in England learns the lesson of self-renunciation, which is *the* great lesson taught by S. Mary in her reply to the message of God, thousands read the inspired record without a thought that a perfect example is there set before them, and a lesson given which each must answer for not learning. Living as they do in an artificial atmosphere, born of ages of civilization which is yearly becoming more false and more hollow, when purity and truth are dying out and their opposites coming in as a flood, invading the courts of queens and emperors, the domestic hearth, the nursery of the child, and even the sanctuaries of the Church of the living God,—those who are by Baptism, daughters of the Church would do well to study the character of "Mary, the Mother of Jesus," and learn from her how to become true handmaids of the Lord.

More than eighteen hundred years have passed away since the words, " Be it unto me according to thy word," were spoken by the Virgin, but through the centuries they have been echoed and re-echoed by all God's true children, who have learned to love the highest good by casting out self, and willing that God's Will, and not their own, shall reign supreme, and shape their course in time and their destiny in the long hereafter.

When S. Mary is next mentioned by the inspired writers, she is traversing the hill-country of Judea in haste, in order to visit her cousin Elizabeth, of whom the Angel Gabriel had spoken, and predicted that she, in her old age, should have a son.

In this scene of the great drama, all is
what the world calls supernatural; and
as in imagination we enter the house of
Zacharius, mark the effect of the salutation
of the Blessed Virgin, and listen to the
words which fell from the lips of Elizabeth,
we seem to have the spirit world laid bare
before our mortal eyes, and we realize the
awful fact of its nearness, above, around,
within us, and that the supernatural
holds all that we call natural in its em-
brace.

Elizabeth's mind is supernaturally enlightened, and as her bodily eye rests
upon her cousin Mary, the eye of faith
sees in her the Mother of God, and she
spake with a loud voice, and said, "Blessed
art thou among women, and blessed is the
fruit of thy womb. And whence is this to
me, that the Mother of my Lord should
come to me? For, lo, as soon as the voice

of thy salutation sounded in mine ears, the babe leaped in my womb for joy."

Marvellous was the life of the great prophet S. John the Baptist, of whom we thus read, before he was born into the world, as moved and sanctified by the immediate Presence of the unborn Christ ; testifying to the working of God's unseen laws.

Strange it is that man should pride himself, as so many do in these days of critical investigation and extended knowledge, on disbelieving all that he cannot see or understand, when his own inventions disclose so many wonders beyond his reach, and his intellect shows him that there are vast fields in which he cannot work by reason of his limited powers—forces in nature which he can neither comprehend nor control, and, above all, the spirit within him, of which it may be said that, while knowing so much, he knows but little.

As in the material world we come to a
point where the connecting link between
the animal and vegetable kingdoms is not
discernible, so it is with the invisible part
of creation.   None can draw the line and
say, "Here instinct ends and reason begins,"
or, "This point marks the separation of sen-
tient and unconscious nature : " nor can the
highest intellect discover where matter
ends and spirit begins, for they are so
closely blended together, and act upon one
another in such wonderful and various
ways, that it is impossible to separate
them ; yet they are perfectly distinct, and
man has in himself the clearest demonstra-
tion of the fact which so many men of
high intellectual powers profess to ignore.

Earth and sea and sky, spirit and matter,
disease and death were subject to the God-
man.   These miracles, so called because
they are manifestations of laws which man

does not understand, are denied and have
been denied by sceptics of every age : yet
they are, we cannot doubt, but higher
developments of the same unchanging
laws of an unchangeable and omniscient
Lawgiver, the Creator and Fashioner of
the universe; and those who are content
to cast in their lot with S. Paul, and to
confess with him that here "we see
through a glass darkly," feel that in the
record of the meeting of S. Mary and S.
Elizabeth the Holy Spirit has revealed
the mysterious working of God's laws,
Spirit acting upon matter—the Spirit of
God Incarnate inspiring His as yet unborn great forerunner.

As in the Annunciation we saw in the
person of S. Mary how "perfect love
casteth out fear," so now in the hill-
country her example teaches the same
lesson. The supernatural has no terrors

for her. The sudden appearance of an angel, the inspired salutation of Elizabeth, seem to come to her but as the bright shining of the sun, or as a deep melodious chord falls upon the ear. She sees and hears, and welcomes both as messages from her God; and inspired by the Holy Spirit she sings her song of triumph, which the Church has made her own and re-echoed for nearly two thousand years.

From the "Magnificat" we learn more of the character of the Virgin than from any other revelation of her which is vouch-safed to us. To magnify the Lord, to rejoice in God her Saviour, is her first thought and act after being saluted as the Mother of God, followed by a deep feeling of humility. A sense of her own lowliness is an abiding principle, and there is no thought of self even in her exulting words, "All generations shall call me blessed;"

for all glory is ascribed to Him that is mighty, Who had magnified her, and Whose name is Holy. So it has always been and so it will ever be with the meek and lowly of heart who are pronounced "blessed" by the Saviour, as also are "they which do hunger and thirst after righteousness," for they are " filled with good things," when " the rich " are "sent empty away."

Little did S. Mary think that her song would be sung on earth by successive generations until the end of time, or that her words breathed forth among the hills of Judea gave to the world a perfect example of exalted humility; for they were an unconscious portraiture of herself, an embodiment of the grace given indeed by God, but made her own by the exercise of her own free will.

As we read the " Magnificat " thought

travels back to an age long past, when the Word of the Lord came to man, and it was written, "Thus saith the high and lofty One that inhabiteth eternity, Whose name is Holy. I dwell in the high and holy place, with him also who is of a contrite and humble spirit ; " and to the time when the Saviour sat on the Mount and the Beatitudes fell from His gracious lips, — for as we read of the "poor in spirit," "the meek," " the merciful," "the peacemakers," "the pure in heart," do we not see that all these qualities combined to form the character of her who was pre-eminently blessed among women, and who was in an especial manner a type of the Church, and the archetype which God has given to the world for the daughters of the Church to study and to imitate.

We may not, in this scene in the life

of S. Mary, pass over without notice the record that Elizabeth's salutation, "Blessed art thou among women," was given with a loud voice; for, as Isaac Williams says, "the loud voice, as the loud voice of our Lord at His death, indicates that it is with Divine not human power that she spake; using the very same words as the Angel had used to her before, for it was the same Holy Spirit that spake in both, declaring the same both by angels and men."

To these words may be added another thought in connection with the foregoing remarks on the union of the supernatural with the natural. The loud voice would seem to indicate God's purpose to make man feel that, powerful as He is in His works which are seen by men, His unseen power is greater; and that the evidence of things revealed by the Holy Spirit is far above that of sight and touch.

And here we are reminded of our Lord's words to S. Thomas: " Because thou hast seen thou hast believed; blessed are those who have not seen and yet have believed." So it is, that until "faith is lost in sight— not our present limited sight, but the full and perfect sight we shall have when we are made like unto the Son of God— the special benediction rests upon those whose faith grasps higher and deeper verities than the things of sense and sight.

As the higher part of man realizes day by day the illimitable power of its cap- abilities, so the powers of his visible and material part become dwarfed in his esti- mation; the unseen to mortal vision becomes real and lasting; the seen, as real indeed, but only transitory, to be cared for and kept undefiled as long as it lasts,—in short, to be regarded as a precious casket, but of lesser value than the jewel it contains.

It is to those who, by receiving God's word without doubts or disputings, are so spiritually enlightened as to bring home to their minds as a reality the immaterial part of their nature, that the words of man's great Father so often recur; and as the Church repeats them year by year, and those words, "Come, let us reason together," fall upon the ear, whenever they strike deep into the heart, the grand diapason is touched, and man not only feels but knows that harmony is God's law, and that man was in very deed and truth made in the image of God— made to live in and through and by Him, to be one with Him, and that man's highest happiness must ever consist in the entire fulfilment of his simplest duty, viz., willing that *his* will shall be in perfect accord with God's Will—the receptacle, as it were, of that Will, a sort of treasure-house, always open to receive the riches of grace which

are ever flowing from the Source of all
good, from whom the waves of light are
ever rolling, revealing clearer and clearer
the depths of the wisdom, and justice, and
mercy of God.

They, who use reason rightly, are subject
by reason to God, and consequently find
themselves drawn closer and closer to Him;
yet is their freedom of choice and action
in no way curtailed; it seems rather to
increase than to diminish, and greater
nearness to God only makes man realize
that "His service is perfect freedom." It
needs must be so; for if there be a God,
what limit can there be to His freedom of
action and power? or what limit can there
be to the freedom of those who choose to
be the sons of God? For they are of one
mind and one spirit; one in aim and desire.
Strength is made perfect in weakness, and
man's weakness is transformed into the

power of God whenever the words, "Thy will be done," proceed from the heart, and the utterance of the lips is but the echo of the harmony vibrating between heaven and earth.

A perfect illustration of this truth is seen in the perfect Man, Christ Jesus our Lord. "Not my will but Thine be done" are the notes which form the grand harmonious chord in the music of heaven, telling of the highest reasoning intelligence so subjecting the perfect human will as to make it one with the Divine Will. "Behold the handmaid of the Lord," is S. Mary's refrain; and England's daughters would do well to take it up in days when old landmarks are being swept away, and the tempter of mankind is raising his old warcry, "Disobey God's commands, use the power you have, and ye shall be as gods, knowing good and evil."

In the third scene in which S. Mary is
presented to our view, we see her led by
S. Joseph, weary with a long journey, and
seeking shelter but finding none, save in
the stable of a village inn, that stable
being, according to the account of Origen
and of other early writers, a cave in the
rock. The journey had been undertaken in
obedience to the decree issued by Cæsar
Augustus for all the world to be taxed, and
so it came to pass that the path of obedience
led S. Mary to the birth-place of her great
ancestor David, the son of Jesse, the Beth-
lehemite, where she ·gave birth to the
Saviour of the world.

In the stable-cave at Bethlehem the Child
Jesus was born—Jesus, the Son of Mary,
the handmaid of the Lord; Jesus, Who
came unto His own, and His own received
Him not; Who was wrapped in swathing-
bands and laid in a manger; Who, as He

increased in wisdom and s ature, was subject to His Mother and to His foster-father,
thus giving to the world a perfect example
of humility and obedience. Yet of this
same Jesus and of His lowly birth-place it
had been written, "Out of thee shall come
forth a Governor who shall rule My people
Israel," "Whose goings forth have been
from old, from everlasting."

"The High and Lofty One Who inhabiteth eternity," goes forth from Beth-
'lehem as the Son of Mary, who in the
City of David was a stranger and pilgrim,
so poor that none took any account of
her and S. Joseph being of royal extrac-
tion. The fact that both were of the house
and lineage of David failed to secure them
a temporary home in David's own city;
and the men of that generation who had
congregated together at Bethlehem, in
obedience to the command of a Roman

emperor, were blind to the stupendous event consummated in their midst.

The "Holy, Holy, Holy, Lord God of Hosts, heaven and earth are full of Thy Glory; glory be to Thee, O Lord Most High," rang through the courts of heaven when S. Mary laid the Infant Saviour on His manger-throne. The "Trisagion" was not heard in the Cave of the Nativity; but an Angel of the Lord appeared to shepherds who were "keeping watch over their flock by night. And the glory of the Lord shone round about them. And the Angel said, 'Behold, I bring you good tidings of great joy; for unto you is born this day in the City of David a Saviour, which is Christ the Lord. And this shall be a sign unto you : Ye shall find the Child wrapped in swaddling clothes, lying in a manger.'"

Another wonderful unveiling this was of

the spirit world; and the shepherds, we are told, "were sore afraid;" but they had yet greater things to see and hear, for suddenly there was with the Angel a multitude of the Heavenly Host, praising God, and saying, "Glory to God in the Highest, and on earth peace, goodwill towards men."

All who study the Holy Scriptures must be struck with the frequent mention of Angels. In fact, the Bible is full of them; and yet in these latter days those who deny that the visible Church is the pillar and ground of the truth, God's living witness on earth, the only safe keeper and expounder of His written Word, while taking the Bible as their sole rule of faith, seem to regard all that inspired writers have told us of Angels as revelations of a time long past, in which mankind has now no interest. There is no apparent difference on this subject in those who, having set up the idol of private judgment, are a law unto themselves, and the materialists, who affect to believe only what they see; for each treats all practical belief in the unseen universe as a vain superstition.

The true members of the Church, in this as in every other age, believe that they have a deep, real, and individual interest in all that is revealed of the invisible creation; and the more they search into these things and ponder them in their hearts, as the Holy Virgin of Nazareth did, the more harmony they see in the works of God.

In all ages God has allowed Angels to become visible to man, with whom they are closely allied. Unlike as Angels are to us in most things, they are like us in others; they are rational, intelligent Beings, higher, holier, purer than we are, but worshippers of the same God and universal Father, and, as the Bible tells us, " they are all ministering spirits sent forth to minister to them who shall be heirs of salvation." As one has written, " Whatever man does, there are Angels assisting, defending, protecting, instructing him. By God's appointment they were the guardians of Eden against man's re-entrance there after he had committed sin ; but to him outside Eden they have been ever comforters and succourers."

It is an old belief, old as the oldest records of God's ancient people, that each of mankind has his Angel Guardian, and it is the belief of each member of Christ's Church who holds "*the* Faith " in its entirety, that each child is consigned at its Baptism to the special care of one of the Holy Angels. We know that S. Mary manifested no surprise at the appearance of an Angel, from which fact we may fairly assume that her knowledge of the Jewish Scriptures made the visible presence of one no strange thing to her. That she realized their nearness, and that she had that faith which S. Paul defines to be "the substance of things hoped for, the evidence of things not seen," we cannot doubt; hence her calmness and fearlessness under all circumstances.

Oh that the daughters of the Church would, in these days of unreality and indifferentism, strive earnestly after this faith! Could they be cold in heart and thankless for all the mercies of their daily lives, if they realized only one of those mercies—the presence of a pure Angel, ever near, ever watching them, sorrowing when they do wrong, rejoicing when they do right? Whether they believe it or not the great fact remains, that no one is ever *alone*; the Angels of God surround

us night and day; the ladder which Jacob
saw in a vision has not been removed, it
still connects heaven and earth, and
Angels are ever ascending and descending
on errands of love and mercy.

In Bethlehem the shepherds found the
Babe lying in a manger; and while they
told to the Virgin Mother the wonderful
story of the adoring Angels exulting in
the exceeding greatness and lowliness of
Him who had taken upon Him the
form of a servant, the world outside the
Cave went on its way, not knowing that
the long-expected Messiah of the favoured
people of God had come, and that the
Virgin Mother, of whom their great prophet Isaiah had written, was cradling the
Saviour of the world among the beasts of
the stall.

Oh, proud world! what hast thou
ever done for the children of God? Even

what thou didst to God Himself when He took upon Him our flesh and dwelt among us. Thou hast given hate for love, cursing for blessing, and ingratitude for mercies innumerable as the stars. Thou hast persecuted the faithful in all ages; thou hast drunk the blood of the martyrs; thou hast tried to destroy Christ's Church, as thou didst crucify the Head of the Church outside the walls of Jerusalem. Thou hast ever hated the story of the Cross; nevertheless no chapter of it has been lost; each page is treasured in the hearts of all who like S. Mary ponder all things, written for their learning, in their hearts.

Not in a cave is the next scene of the great drama, but in a gorgeous temple, even the Temple at Jerusalem; and here thought is at once arrested and our attention called to the lesson which the magnificence of the Temple built according to the plan of its Almighty Architect was intended to teach mankind. Truly our English Hooker has well summed up that lesson in his own quaint and forcible words, "God has nowhere told us that He likes to be served beggarly;" and no country in the world is richer in buildings which testify that the lesson which God Himself taught Solomon has been learned by the Christians of later days, than England. Her cathedrals are something more than grand old buildings; they are stately poems, lofty imaginings embodied in stone. Their foundations are deep and strong, and the superstructure is typical of the religion that was to be taught beneath their roofs. When gazing upon such buildings, the words of a poet recur to memory, and we feel that—

" They dreamt not of a perishable home
Who thus could build."

When those Cathedrals which stud our land
were raised, men were few in number
and widely scattered. Those Houses of
God were built for Him and for His
glory, and so the builders laid stone upon
stone richly wrought with curious and
significant device ; higher and higher they
raised the clustered columns, crowning
them with rich capitals from which sprang
the glorious arches and groined roof ; and
as they went from nave to chancel, from
chancel to Sanctuary, the mind of the
designer soared to a yet loftier height,
and the handiwork became more elaborate,
—as was meet—for there the Altar Throne
of the Lamb of God was to stand when the
House was builded and made ready for
the presence of God.

And behind the Altar of the Lamb we

always find, in these old Churches, the Lady Chapel. The position of it seems to indicate that it was intended by the master minds which designed our Cathedrals as typical of the Blessed Virgin's hidden life on earth. They honoured her as the Mother of their Lord, and built her chapel where the first rays of the rising sun would stream through the eastern window and light up the slender marble columns and the delicate tracery with which they loved to adorn the place they dedicated to her in God's House, in humble imitation, as it were, of the Christian gifts and graces with which God adorned her.

Yet was that Chapel not open to the common gaze of all: it was built *behind* the High Altar; and always in that sacred seclusion there is a smaller Altar, on which to offer that "pure Sacrifice" of which the prophet Malachi wrote—even Him Whom the Blessed Virgin cradled in her arms; Him on Whom the Holy Spirit descended in the form of a dove; Him, the hidden God of the Eucharist, Who gives Himself to all who stretch forth their hands and open their hearts to receive Him.

Wonderful are the ways of God—most wonderful in their perfect harmony. All His attributes are blended together, and are made manifest in their working among the children of men. The Holy Virgin of Israel was the work of His Hands; with His free Spirit, He gave her freedom of choice and power if she *willed* to use her freedom aright, to choose the good and refuse evil; and so it was that when forty days had elapsed since the birth of the child Jesus, His blessed Mother, accompanied by S. Joseph, took Him to Jerusalem to present Him to the Lord, and to fulfil the Jewish law in her own person. No privilege did she claim that was not accorded to other women. Implicit obedience in all that was lawful was the environment in which every grace that adorned her was set ; and Faith, Adoration, Devotion, Humility and Thanksgiving were all manifest in her when she made her offerings in the Temple.

No throng of courtiers crowded the aisles of that magnificent building, which the Holy Child in later days called His Father's House, when He was carried into it in His Mother's arms. Many doubtless were there, coming in from the distractions of the world and returning to them, without having seen more than an aged man and a young mother fulfilling the Law. So God's opportunities are missed by those whose thoughts and affections are set on earthly things; while those who watch, and pray, and look for light, have it.

There was a man in Jesusalem whose name was Simeon ; he was just and devout, and was waiting for the consolation of Israel. To him it was revealed by the Holy Ghost that he should not see death before he had seen the Lord's Christ. And he came by the Spirit into the Temple : and when the Child Jesus was brought in, he took Him up in his arms, and blessed God, and said, "Lord, now lettest Thou Thy servant depart in peace, according to Thy word. For mine eyes have seen Thy salvation, which Thou hast prepared before the face of all people ; a light to lighten the Gentiles, and the glory of Thy people Israel." Then Simeon blessed Joseph and Mary ; but in blessing he told the Mother of the sword that should pierce her own soul.

Another is added to the group—Anna, a prophetess, a widow of great age, who served God with fastings and prayers day and night. She likewise gave thanks unto the Lord. And then, when all things had been performed according to the law of the Lord, the Holy Family returned to their own city Nazareth.

There is one great lesson which S. Mary's conduct on this occasion teaches, which is much needed in these days; for there are many in the world who say that Christ having fulfilled the law for us, and offered Himself for us, nothing more than a belief in Him is necessary on our part, and that no offerings we can make are of any avail towards securing our salvation. This they say, although their professed Guide tells them to *work out* their salvation with fear and trembling.

But we need not wander from the example of S. Mary, to ascertain what God requires of us. We may learn from what she did that God does require our offerings.

If He did not, the Blessed Virgin would not have made any. If she, illuminated by the Holy Spirit, performed as a simple duty on her part all that the Jewish law required, how shall those who set aside and refuse to obey the law of Christ's Church be justified?

With far less light than we have, the Patriarchs of the old dispensation obeyed the commands of God, in simple faith that He Who issued the command knew best what was right and good for the creature He had created. We are told that when Noah made his offerings "the Lord smelled a sweet savour;" that is, the incense of a willing mind, a loving heart, and the sacrifice of self; and when S. Mary made her priceless offering and presented her Divine Son to His Father in heaven, she offered also a pair of turtle doves.

How different this to the spirit of the

age in which we live! The men and women of to-day boast of having the Spirit, and in their exaltation they despise forms and ceremonies, and the godly discipline of earlier days. What can those who are drawn by God's grace into some calm retreat where the din of the world ceases to be heard, and the teachings of the Holy Spirit are borne in upon the mind, what can they think of the choice of those who have set themselves up as judges of God's plan of salvation for man, when they compare the downward path in which their choice leads them, with the way in which the Virgin Mary walked? Surely that it is one full of hidden dangers—not only because it is the opposite path to the one taken by her who was "full of Grace," but also because God has willed from the beginning that the Grace which He bestows, and without which no man can

be saved, shall be cherished and used by
man in His appointed way.

God will not have His gift left like a
diamond in the mine, unseen, uncared for,
but He has willed that it shall shine forth
in man's setting of good works, and that
the fruits of the Spirit shall cluster round
it and make it manifest to the world. "Let
your light so shine before men that they
may see your good works and glorify your
Father which is in heaven," were some of
the words which fell from the lips of the
Saviour as He sat and taught His disciples
on the Mount of Beatitudes; and through
the veil in which God in His wisdom has
enfolded the Virgin, we see issuing rays of
light which testify to her fulfilment of this
Divine precept — so perfect a fulfilment
that, veiled though she be, we see that
she is in very deed and in truth the "Light-
clad Mother of Light."

In the next scene, rays of light from a strange bright star are resting upon the lowly abode in Bethlehem, which sheltered the Holy Family, and before the door are the wise men from the East. One has said, "At the same time, Christ was declared to the Jews by an Angel, to the Gentiles by a star. The wise men were employed in watching stars, by a star God called them: so He mercifully uses the means open to each of us for our call." Many are called, few answer; but the wise men delayed not to follow the leading of the star, nor paused in search of Him Whom they came to worship, until it came and stood over where the young Child was.

Then "they rejoiced with exceeding great joy." And they made ready their costly presents which they had brought with them from their own country; "and when they were come into the house, they saw the

young Child with Mary His Mother, and
fell down and worshipped Him : and when
they had opened their treasures, they
presented unto Him gifts, gold, and frankincense, and myrrh." The best of all they
possessed they gave as unto a King, and
with those earthly gifts, something far more
precious in the sight of God—adoring love,
the prayer of faith and mortification of self,
of which the gold, the frankincense, and
myrrh were but the outward symbols. Yet
were the symbols necessary signs of the
inward spiritual grace. Man is made up
of body and Spirit; the universe, of
material and immaterial; and it is in the
blending together of each that we see the
perfection of God's works.

We are left to imagine the feelings of
the Blessed Virgin as she stood or knelt
with the Eastern Sages by the side of her
Child. To her and to them, the scene,

passing so quickly, as all bright moments upon earth do, must have been as the glory of the setting sun followed by a dark stormy night ; for during the darkness that succeeded the shining of the Star of the Nativity the wise men, being warned of God in a dream, departed to their own country. And when they were departed the Angel of the Lord appeared unto Joseph in a dream, saying, " Arise, and take the young Child and His Mother, and flee into Egypt, and be thou there until I bring thee word."

How little are the ways of God's saints like the ways of the men of this world ! Joseph arose ; he took no thought of the morrow, but simply obeyed the command of the Lord. " He took the young Child and His Mother by night, and departed into Egypt," and was there until God again sent His Angel, who appeared to him, as before, in a dream, and directed him to return to the land of Israel, "for," the Angel added, "they are dead who sought the young Child's life."

No sooner is the command given than it is obeyed. Joseph arose and took the young Child and His Mother, and came and dwelt in a city called Nazareth. There, where God willed the Holy Family to dwell, and where He cast a veil over the life of the Blessed Mother which no mortal can raise, we leave them with the prayer that we may learn the lesson of obedience which every incident in the brief summary of such stupendous events as the Holy Spirit has revealed is calculated to teach us. To obey is better than sacrifice, and blessed are they who choose, as S. Mary ever did, that good part which shall not be taken away from them.

Twelve years pass away before the Blessed Virgin is again presented to our view. She and S. Joseph then take the Holy Child with them to Jerusalem at the Feast of the Passover ; and S. Luke tells us that "when they had fulfilled the days, as they returned, the Child Jesus tarried behind in Jerusalem; and Joseph and His Mother knew not of it." But thinking He was in the company, they proceeded a day's journey, and were seeking Him among their kinsfolk and acquaintance. "And when they found Him not, they returned to Jerusalem, seeking Him." Sorrowfully the Holy Mother searched for her Child.

It would seem from the sacred narrative that at this time S. Mary's feelings as a woman overcame the higher nature implanted within her. This is but a beautiful and merciful illustration of the fact that, though so richly endued with Grace, she was in all respects a true woman, liable to be cast down and to shrink from the touch of adversity.

For three days the Mother thought only of Jesus as *her* Child, and she looked for Him in Jerusalem and found Him not. Then she and S. Joseph repaired to the Temple, doubtless to pray, and there in His Father's House they found Him sitting in the midst of the Doctors, both hearing and asking them questions. Even then, though they were themselves amazed, and saw that all who listened to the Holy Child "were astonished at His understanding and answers," the Mother, in her grief at the temporary loss of her Son, still looked not behind the veil of the flesh, but said unto Him, "Child, why hast Thou thus done unto us? Behold, Thy father and I have sought Thee sorrowing."

Solemnly, but softly as dew from heaven

falls upon earth's grass and flowers, fell
the words from the lips of the Son of
God, "How is it that ye sought Me? Wist
ye not that I must be about My Father's
business?" In these words are manifested
the majesty of God and the tenderness of
the Child. He asserts that He has work
to do which belongs by sovereign right and
power exclusively to Him, and with which
no human agency may interfere. The
principle embodied in the words, "My
meat is to do the will of Him that sent
Me, and to finish His work;" "I must
work the works of Him that sent Me while
it is day," was the Saviour's rule of life
from first to last, when He could say, "I
have finished the work which Thou gavest
Me to do."

S. Ambrose says, "There are in Christ
two generations; the one that of His
Father, the other of His Mother: that

of the Father Divine, but that of the Mother which descends to our labour and usage. And therefore those things which take place beyond nature, beyond age, beyond custom, are not to be ascribed to human virtues but to be referred to Divine powers."

And so, we may not doubt, the blessed Mother understood the words spoken by the Son of God; for we are told that she "kept all these sayings in her heart;" and the gentle reproof which reminded her that He acknowledged no earthly father, by recalling to memory past wonders must have brought vividly before her the fact that she was acting a part in a great mystery, too high and deep for her to comprehend except as it should be revealed to her by Divine grace and power.

As her Child, Jesus was subject unto her; He was ever a perfect example of filial

obedience ; and they who realize the weakness of human nature—and none realize
that weakness with such clearness and in-
tensity as God's greatest saints do—wonder
not that in S. Mary's sorrow for the loss
of her Child she should forget for the
moment all else, and that her sorrow
should bring a passing cloud over her
faith, for such is life on earth—alternate
darkness and light, cloud and sunshine ;
but the rain-drops which fall in the sun-
light bring before us the bow of promise,
and we ponder these things in our hearts,
and go on our way rejoicing, with the
" bright and morning Star " leading us on
along the royal road of the Holy Cross to
the gates of the Golden City.

This episode in the life of the Virgin
should teach all that it is useless to seek
for Christ in the world. He is not there ;
He was not found by Dives : and the

daughters of His Church in England, who, like Dives, are clothed in purple and fine linen and fare sumptuously every day, are in greater danger of losing the "Pearl of great price," than others who, having fewer riches and honours, have also fewer temptations.

We are not told that Dives was a blasphemer, or immoral; only that, in the midst of his wealth and ease and enjoyment of the good things of this world, he forgot God and did not minister to the wants of the poor. And is the gay, thoughtless, fashionable woman of the world, who flutters, as a moth around the flame of a candle, on the confines of evil, in a safer position than Dives? Is she not casting in her lot with the "foolish virgins?" When does she find time to trim her lamp and feed with the oil of prayer the ght that was kindled when the

sign of the Cross was made upon her fore-
head, and she was made a member of
Christ, a child of God, and an inheritor
of the kingdom of heaven? When does
she pass even a fleeting hour in imitating
S. Mary, and pondering the teaching of her
Saviour in her heart? Alas! the world
leaves no time for meditation : early youth
is passed in preparations for shining in
"society," in making white the outside of
the sepulchre ; and when that is accomplished, the plunge is made into that sea of
pleasure and dissipation whose waves are
never at rest, where no calm ever comes,
and where the soft breathings of the Holy
Spirit are rarely felt.

At the close of the last record of the
childhood of Jesus which inspired writers
give, they tell us that "He went down
with them" (S. Mary and S. Joseph),
"and came to Nazareth, and was subject

F

unto them. . . . And Jesus increased in wisdom and stature, and in favour with God and Man."

In a few words we have the perfect out-line of the home-life at Nazareth. Only one detail is added, and that is a revelation of the Virgin, "His Mother kept all these sayings in her heart." If S. Mary, a daughter of the House of David, honoured by God, raised above all other daughters of Eve when the Angel proclaimed her "blessed among women," if she thus spent her life on earth, the short transitory school-life which is designed to prepare each member of the human family for the higher life beyond the grave,—and if our state in the next world depends, as we know it does, on the use we make of talents and opportunities during our brief life in this world,—would not the daughters of kings and nobles, in these days when

all things seem to indicate that " the Judge
is at the door," do well to take heed and
imitate the pattern woman, " Mary, the
Mother of Jesus " ?

Just what we make ourselves by edu-
cating the higher spiritual part of our
nature, what we *are* when we enter the
valley of the shadow of death, that we shall
be when, at the end of the dark valley, the
spirit leaves the earthly tabernacle in which
it has dwelt during its time of trial upon
earth. There is no pause, no break in the
career of an immortal spirit ; and the
Gate of Death is but a station where we
have to change the conditions of an eternal,
progressive state. Youth and beauty quickly
pass away, health and strength fail, and all
that is earthly decays, but that part of man
which rules the body does not grow old
and decay, it lives on for ever in that place
for which it was fitted by the deeds done

in the body ; and those who follow closest
in the steps of the Blessed Virgin on earth
will, we cannot doubt, be nearest to her
in glory.

At a marriage in Cana of Galilee we
next see S. Mary, where she is spoken of
as the " Mother of Jesus." There also is
Jesus and His disciples.

Contemplativeness is a marked feature in
the character of the Blessed Virgin, un-
obtrusiveness is another, and therefore we
look below the surface of the scene sketched
for us by the hand of S. John, in order to
discover what lesson is deducible from the
prominent part which S. Mary is repre-
sented as taking in it.   Well versed as she
doubtless was in the Jewish Scriptures, it
would seem that when at the marriage feast
the wine failed, knowing who her Son was
in an especial manner, and remembering
also the incidents of His wonderful life, it

may very well be, that the multiplying of the barley loaves by Elisha, and other incidents in the Old Testament occurred to her mind. However that may be, she departs from her customary reserve, and addressing Jesus, she said, "They have no wine." No public miracle had Jesus yet wrought, nor are we told that He had worked miracles while He dwelt at Nazareth, but the Mother's words indicate a belief on her part that her Son had power to supply what was needed.

Harsh and strange in their English garb do the words uttered by the lowly Jesus sound to us ; but the Blessed Virgin's deep contemplation of all that was spoken by the Saviour, caused her to regard His words as "spirit" and as "life," and her faith in Him was made manifest by her immediately saying to the servants, "Whatsoever He may say unto you, do it." "Here," as Isaac Williams says, "notwithstanding the cloud that veils the Blessed Mother from our view, she breaks forth as a type of the Church, teaching obedience to Christ as the beginning of all our hopes; as if saying to us all, ' Whatsoever He saith unto you, do it,' and leave to Him the issue. May it not be that when the 'time' is fully 'come,' the Church shall thus ask in faith, and on the obedience of her ministers to His command, Christ shall work miracles, converting poor earthly elements into the sacramental riches of His Kingdom?"

The wishes of the Blessed Virgin were manifest from her words; and Jesus, as in time past when the gracious promise was given, " Before they call I will answer, and while they are yet speaking I will hear," was ready to grant them, and to anticipate the time for the manifestation of His power;

but He waited until by her faith and obedience the light which burned so brightly in His Mother should shine before men, and then, for the great love He bore her, He granted all her desire, and, turning to the servants, He said unto them, " ' Fill the waterpots with water,' and they filled them up to the brim." Again Jesus spoke, " ' Draw out now, and bear unto the Governor of the feast.' And they bare it : " not water but wine. Wonderful transformation, wrought by God in answer to faith, obedience, and prayer ! The Blessed One, at whose suggestion the miracle was wrought, is quickly enfolded in the veil which hides her from the world ; and even those who would sit with her at the feet of Jesus, lose sight of her. All we are told is that, after the marriage feast, she went down to Capernaum with Jesus, and His brethren, and His disciples.

" Ask and ye shall receive," and " According to your faith be it unto you," are the promises which form the sequence to the marriage scene at Cana ; and the lesson we learn from the harmonious whole is the infinite value of intercessory prayer. Never can it fail ; and blessed are they whose faith is like the faith of the Mother of Jesus, strong enough to move the Arm of Him who has all power in heaven and on earth.

That faith—" the substance of things hoped for, the evidence of things not seen ; " the strong unwavering faith of the Confessors and Martyrs of earlier days ; the faith which S. Mary had—is what is wanted in these days. " Ye have not, because ye ask not ; " and man asks not, because he has no faith. Faith in the Hearer and Answerer of prayer ; faith in an ever-present Father by Whom even the

hairs of our heads are numbered ; faith in
the Sacraments of the Church, the new birth
in Baptism, the Gift of the Holy Ghost
by the laying on of hands, the power of
the keys, and the Presence of Christ in
the Sacrament of the Altar, is dead in the
hearts of the great mass of mankind.

The Wisdom of God is accounted foolish-
ness by the world ; and those who withdraw
from the ways of the world, and strive to
walk in the old paths where the saints of
other days sought and found what made
them wise unto salvation, are laughed at,
as S. Paul was, and are said to be mad.
Nevertheless the Word of God standeth
sure, the prayer of faith shall be answered,
and at the last great day it will be seen
what the " saints' prevailing prayer " has
wrought for that proud world, and for
many of those who, when youth and health
and riches were theirs, made a mock of

prayer, regarded God's Ordinances as useless forms, and His holy days a weariness.

Many of those mockers, in the evening of life, when the shadows are lengthening, and what was once a pleasure to them is pleasure no longer, will *wish* to pray, wish for faith to pray; and that wish, if not stifled by hard wilful unbelief, is the turning into a better way, where the power to pray will be granted by Him Who waits to be gracious. The last great day may prove that the wish to pray, the first voluntary step in the path that leadeth to eternal life, was given in answer to the effectual fervent prayer of one of God's righteous servants.

"And shall not God avenge His own elect who cry day and night unto Him?" Will He not arise and scatter the enemies of His Church in these last evil days, and

shelter the Bride, the Lamb's Wife, under
the shadow of His wings, in answer to the
prayers of the faithful, as He shielded
the Virgin Mother, the Archetype of the
Church, during her sojourn upon earth?

Once more, and only once, the veil is
raised, and that but for a moment, until
it is flung aside to disclose the awful scene
on Calvary. Jesus had been preaching to
the people, and it was said to Him, "'Thy
Mother and Thy brethren stand without,
desiring to see Thee.' And He answered
and said unto them, 'My mother and My
brethren are these that hear the word of
God, and do it'"

In these words of our Lord we have a
brief description of the true members of
His Church from its foundation to the end
of time; and they are calculated to inspire
each son and daughter of the Church with
that courage which S. Mary had when

she stood by the Cross on which the Son of man was dying, but from which the "Strong Son of God" bent down His thorn-crowned Head to comfort His Mother and give one more proof of His immortal love.

As with the Head, so with the members; and the children of the Church, few in number compared with the howling multitude who are crying, "Down with her, down with her, even to the ground," need all the faith and the courage which faith gives, that were so conspicuously displayed at the foot of the Cross, to enable them to persevere unto the end.

But even as S. Mary's faith enabled her to stand during the three hours' agony, so they who believe that Christ is on our Altars stand by *them*, and have no fears. Where He is there must be safety; for He Who calmed the waves and stilled the wind when the ship was tossed to and fro on the lake of Gennesareth, can and will in His own good time manifest His almighty power again ; and when that moment comes, the faithful will hear the words, " Peace, be still," and then they will see the Ark of Christ's Church unharmed by the storm that is now raging around her, and re-member the promise that the gates of hell shall not prevail against her.

More than eighteen hundred years ago, outside the walls of Jerusalem, on Mount Calvary, stood a Cross. On it was the Saviour of the world, and at the foot of the Cross was His Mother. The hour foretold by Simeon, when the sword should pierce through her soul, had come ; she had trodden the Via Dolorosa and was stand-ing, as S. John tells us, by the Cross.

In witnessing the Crucifixion of her Divine Son, she crucified herself. Who can imagine the agony of that hour? Surely only one so " full of grace " as she was could have " stood " firm and resigned to the Will of God, waiting patiently through the awful three hours' darkness upon the dying Saviour, the Child she had carried in her arms, the Son whom God had given to her. She shrank not from the torture of her watch at the foot of the Cross ; and Jesus, whose filial love must have exceeded that of all other sons for their mothers, because He was our perfect pattern in all things, knowing how much she needed consolation, gave it in His last dread hour of mortal suffering.

One of the Fathers has said, " Our Blessed Lord ever bestows more than is demanded of Him, and His grant is always larger than the petition." His Mother asked for nothing, and He commended to her His beloved disciple, S. John, and bade S. John be unto her as a son. Thus He showed His love in providing for her a home on earth, a hiding-place in the desert, a shelter from the storm until the appointed hour should come when the Lily of Israel would be transplanted from earth to heaven, there to reign with Him Who redeemed her for ever and ever.

Very remarkable is the silence of Holy Scripture respecting the Blessed Virgin at this solemn epoch of her life. Of the home to which S. John took her, we are told nothing; all is hushed, like the stillness of a great forest when no breeze stirs the leaves of the trees, when the birds have folded their wings and all nature is sleeping, when the great light which will presently awake creation has withdrawn its shining, and only the far-off light of stars prevents total darkness. When the words went forth, "It is finished," the

veil, never to be raised again in time, falls
over the Virgin Mother, and only from
behind the veil is a voice heard, telling
us that she was watching and praying with
others in Jerusalem. She lives, but no
further revelation of her is vouchsafed.
S. Mary is henceforth concealed from view.

That in proportion to her love for
Jesus, and her faith in and obedience to
Him as the Son of God, she would be
comforted by Him who wept at the grave
of Lazarus, and gave back to the widow of
Nain her only son, none can doubt. That
she whose nearness to Himself was the
cause of her deepest sorrow would be less
favoured than His disciples and the Mag-
dalene, none who receive the Holy Scriptures in their entirety as the inspired Word
of God would for a moment believe ; but
in what way the Mother of the Son of God
was supported and comforted we are not

told, and for man to try to look beyond the veil is as hopeless and unprofitable a task as it would be to enter a dark mine, unaided by light and an infallible guide, to search for a diamond.

To one groping in darkness along an unknown road, every onward step, no matter in what direction that step is taken, is fraught with danger. Man can add nothing to S. Mary's glory by his vain imaginings, and it is certain that he cannot take from it. As the good old monk who gave us the "Imitation of Christ" wrote, "Thou art not the more holy, though thou be commended ; nor the more worthless, though thou be found fault with. What thou art, that thou art ; neither by words canst thou be made greater than what thou art in the sight of God."

Again, S. Paul says, "If we suffer we shall also reign with Him." These words bring

G

suffering and glory very near to each other, and the *soul* that was *pierced* by a sword, must be close to the heart of the " Man of Sorrows." He who was "despised and rejected, and acquainted with grief;" Who " hath borne our griefs, and carried our sorrows;" Who "was wounded for our transgressions and bruised for our iniquities;" Who was "oppressed and afflicted;" "brought as a lamb to the slaughter;" "taken from prison and from judgment;" "cut off out of the land of the living;"—He hath prayed, "Father, I will that they also, whom Thou hast given Me, be with Me where I am." Verily there is no need to look behind the veil in order to do honour to the Mother of our Lord ! That omnipotent prayer of Jesus included His Mother; and when the first heaven and the first earth shall have passed away, and that great city, the holy Jerusalem, shall have descended out of heaven from God, there all those servants of the Lamb who have " His name in their foreheads " will see the Virgin Mother as she is, and reign with her for ever and ever ; and in the light of the Bright and Morning Star, will see also in the over-shadowing of the Virgin's life on earth, as in all God's works and ways from the beginning, infinite wisdom and perfection, the just balance ; and it is when man casts his finite know-ledge and imperfection into one scale or the other, that the straight beam becomes inclined, one scale is lowered and the other elevated and perfect order is destroyed.

It is much in these days of anarchy and development to be members of that portion of Christ's Church which has ever regarded the Blessed Virgin as S. Elizabeth did, as the " Mother of our Lord ; " a Church which has never added to, nor subtracted from

the honour due to her. Individual members
may have done so, but England's Church
never; and every true son and daughter
of that Church will join the author of
"The Christian Year" in singing—

> "Ave Maria! thou whose name
> All but adoring love may claim,
>   Yet may we reach thy shrine.
> For He, thy Son and Saviour, vows
> To crown all lowly lofty brows
>   With love and joy like thine.

> "Bless'd is the womb that bare Him, bless'd
> The bosom where His lips were pressed,
>   But rather bless'd are they
> Who hear His word and keep it well,
> The living homes where Christ shall dwell,
>   And never pass away."

Of the life and character of the Blessed
Virgin enough is revealed in Holy Scripture
to make all who study the events of her
life realize the truth that "to obey is better

than sacrifice." " This is the way, walk ye in it," was the command given ; and to obey that command as S. Mary did, is the only way in which the daughters of England can grow more like her.

The path of obedience may seem hard at first to those who have walked in ways of their own choosing, and the flowers growing in it may seem to have no beauty and no fragrance, the voices that greet their ears when they enter the strait and narrow path may have no music for them, and they may feel the air around them grow chill ; but those who enter the valley in which S. Mary walked with Jesus, will soon find that they are travelling on into light, and in that light all things become new, shadows disappear, and in the warm atmosphere of love the flowers expand and blossom into beauty, and the voices which once sounded harsh and discordant fill the air with melody, and the heart with joy and gladness.

"Speak, Lord, for Thy servant heareth," is the earnest, loving answer which springs from the heart of each true child of God when walking in the King's Highway of the Holy Cross. The yoke of Him Who trode it before them, daily becomes lighter; they feel that His commands are not grievous, and that the duties of life, however hard and irksome they may be, when fulfilled heartily and with a pure intention are changed, when the smile of God rests upon them, into blessings.

Far deeper meaning attaches to every word spoken by the Saviour, than the world dreams of. Saints have not fathomed the depths or measured the heights, but the Catholic Faith embraces all, and makes all of universal application. The daughters of the Church may therefore without presumption consider the words of the dying Saviour, " Behold Thy Mother," as addressed to them individually ; for He had also said, " Whosoever shall do the will of God, the same is my brother, and my sister, and my mother."

Ah, that doing of the will of God! It begins in time, and by the grace of God in the strength of that great and crowning gift, the grace of final perseverance, it never ends. Each child of God, forgetting those things which are behind and reaching forth unto those things which are before, goes on from strength to strength, and when this brief life is over, they who have conquered in the fight on this battle-field of earth will receive the victor's crown and sit down with the blessed Virgin at the marriage supper of the Lamb.

THE END.

PRINTED BY
WILLIAM CLOWES AND SONS, LIMITED,
LONDON AND BECCLES.

www.ingramcontent.com/pod-product-compliance
Lightning Source LLC
Chambersburg PA
CBHW031439270326
41930CB00007B/788